HOW TO KEEP YOUR WOMAN

The handy guide on women,

for men

By

Ophelia Gold

This book belongs to

_____

Date: __/__/__

Authors signature

_____

Introduction

This book covers all bizarre activities, common phrases, and mannerisms from all types of women.

If you feel your woman is malfunctioning, this is the book for you (little clue: it's probably your fault). This guide includes tips for things you should and should never do with your woman. If you refer to this book on a daily basis, it will ensure you live longer, (I mean your relationship will live longer).

Chapters

Am I Fat?

The Art of White Lies

Since the dawn of time, men have often been thrown the most terrifying question known to mankind: "Do I look fat in this?"

The same theme recurs time and time again but worded differently. Such as "Have I gained weight?" "Does this dress look tight on me?" or "Has my bum got bigger?" Each one of these questions was designed to ruin a man's life, and if answered incorrectly, God help you!

The reason a woman asks you this question is that she wants your input. You're more than likely the closest person to her, especially if you live together. She will claim she wants your honest opinion, but this, my friend, is utter bullshit.

There is only ever one answer to any question regarding her weight, and the answer is "No, honey; in fact, have you lost a few pounds?" This will get you out of the danger zone and she'll become sweet as pie to you.

If the actual truth, is she has gained weight, believe me, the phrase "be cruel to be kind" does not apply here. If you're telling her she looks thinner just to please her, know that this is what is referred to as a 'white lie.'

The difference between a lie and a white lie is that one is bad, and the other is good. I know we have been taught that a lie of any nature is entirely unacceptable. It's a double standard.

A white lie is when it's not a life ruining lie, it's a small fib of sorts.

Example

Situation: Her hair looks awful. She's just paid a lot of money at the salon for her new do and she's in love with it and has come back in a fantastic mood. She asks you what you think. You: –

Tell the truth: Ruin her mood, make her feel bad unnecessarily and put a bad atmosphere in the house.

Tell a white lie: Keep her happiness intact, give her false compliments just to inflate her ego to no end. Happy wife = happy husband = happy life.

Disclaimer: Do not become addicted to telling her lies. There is an ENORMOUS difference between lying about being faithful and liking her perfume. Use your common sense. You should know right from wrong by now!

Chocolate

Do not skip past this chapter; it is vital to your life and hers.

Call me crazy, but chocolate has two purposes: romance and medication.

Romance

Obviously, we all know that when it's her birthday or (even better) Valentine's Day, you must buy chocolate. And I don't mean a cheap £1 bar from the corner shop. I'm talking about a quality box of lavish chocolates; I'm not naming brands but think expensive. This shows her that you're seducing and romancing her.

They often go well with her favourite flowers, but don't scrimp on the choccies to afford the flowers (they're nice to look at but they die pretty quickly).

Medication

Yep, you heard me right. Chocolate has been proved to release endorphins in your body, which gives you the sensation of happiness. And I'm sure you'd prefer a happy wife to come home to than a hormonal, crazed psycho.

So, if I were a man, I would keep a stash of chocolate bars handy on my person at all times in case of an emergency. You know just in case you need to tame the beast.

Side note: chocolate has also been known as an aphrodisiac. So, there you have it: chocolate can make her happy, give you a better sex life and it'll let her know you care. In conclusion, chocolate literally fixes everything!

The Time of the Month

Okay, so, we really hate it when we are having an argument with you, and then you recite the worst line known to women:

"What's wrong with you? Are you on your period again?"

Nothing can escalate a heated discussion to a war zone quite as quickly as this piss-take phrase.

(Besides, it's even more embarrassing if you're right!)

The time of the month for women is often referred to as 'The Curse.' Now, this is obviously because once every month, against her wishes, a heavy flow of blood is released from her... body. It leaves her feeling achy, irritable, uncomfortable, unattractive, irrational, moody and emotional. But that's just from her side of things, now from your point of view. I suppose it's still considered a curse for you, because you're the one having to live with her while she's slowly turning into a demon.

We've covered the basic use of chocolate (Remember to keep it on you at all times because you could use it to defend yourself. Throw it at her and then run out of the danger zone. Kind of like throwing a fresh slab of meat at a Rottweiler - it'll buy you time to escape to freedom).

Besides the defence mechanism of chocolate, another trick to carry in your arsenal is to become completely submissive. Do not challenge her on any level, because she will bite your head off, and you will regret it.

If she's in bed rolling around flushing from hot to cold, taking all the covers, then throwing them off the bed in a fit of rage and you're lying there freezing to death...... just die quietly.

Do yourself a favour and don't escalate the situation. I'd say get up, be helpful and ask her if she wants something, a cup of tea, a back rub... anything. And I'm afraid if you don't, she will do a full 360-degree exorcist head spin on your ass.

It's very unfortunate for men at this time of the month, because whether you're being a giant jerk or are genuinely being lovely and helpful, I'm afraid either way you will get the same response from your woman.

So, your only chance of survival is by becoming a mute.

Blend into the shadows. Become the ultimate wall flower.

And should you see her storm out of the room in a rage of fury:

DO NOT FOLLOW HER!

Breathe quietly, don't make eye contact, supply her with chocolate and back rubs, give her compliments (but only when she appears tame... ish) and pretend everything she does is fine with you.

Well, I suppose in simple terms just:

Play dead.

Communication

The basis of all relationships, i.e., family, friends, lovers, colleagues, you name it. It's everywhere. Communication.

Communication is key when we need to keep in touch with people we want to stay in contact with. In a world where social media covers the entire planet, we as people are well adapted to connecting with people in numerous ways.

How is it some marriages end over a severe lack of communication? If you are that person that keeps up with the lives of all your old school friends and know more about them than your own wife, maybe it's time you re-evaluate your priorities. BIG TIME.

Fact

Women love to talk, and if you have a woman in your life, then you already know this.

When you are lacking the sit-down chats with your woman, she will seek this out from fellow females to get this level of stimulating conversation that she blatantly needs.

Girl Talk

If 'Sex and the City' has taught us anything, it's that when women get together, the conversation almost always tends to drift onto the topic of men. A.K.A. you.

If you are being neglectful to your woman, she will conspire against you with her girls. What started off as a small issue has now turned colossal because she has vented all the troubles, she has with you to her entourage of friends. Their inspirational insight on your behaviour will make you the number one enemy in her eyes. Don't let this happen to you. Women united turn into an army and you will surely fail against them.

Avoid this starting, avoid neglect, and, in turn, she will never have to search for support from her troops.

Stay interested in your partner. Over dinner, ask her how her day was. Admittedly, she'll be off on a tangent for hours on end, and she will paint you a full mental picture of her entire day, but it's only because she's animated and excited. She wants to share her life with you.

A relationship is made up of so many parts. Imagine a relationship as a pie chart.

Communication makes up at least 50% of all relationships, which goes to show how important it really is.

Most people are oblivious to this, so now you know, you can spread the wisdom on. It is a common misbelief that love is the most crucial element. I'm sure most of us - *if not all of us* - have loved someone we knew was bad for us. Bad for our mental, emotion, physical or financial health. Love sadly cannot create a successful relationship on its own.

Are You Looking at Her?

(Jealousy)

For as long as the world turns on its axis, women will always be jealous of other women. Envy can creep into their psyche very quickly, from something as simple as one getting higher praise than the other, to envying a stranger with legs longer than hers. Women turn on their own kind often (which is something women really need to work on).

If women can become jealous of each other on their own terms, you can only imagine what your 'subtle' glances to the opposite sex can do to rear the green-eyed monster within her.

As tempting as it is to check out the young hot waitress, consider the following:

Is one little look worth your girlfriend/wife arguing with you for the next three hours?

Will it be worth it when you're sleeping on the couch?

Would it be easier to wait till she's out and then you can look at your Playboy and still keep a serene and peaceful home life?

Is a glance worth a month of being celibate? Because women always know just what punishment to hand out when you fuck up, and, more often than not, it's a severe lack of sex.

Women are fantastic at holding grudges (to our dying day!). Do you really want this cropping into all your future arguments with her?

We've been taught that it's okay to look, but not to touch. Well, when it comes to making a woman jealous, I'd say do neither.

Also, I think men are not at all subtle with their observational tactics. At least when women do it, they are casual about it. They can make it appear as though they were looking for the bathroom as they scan the area. Or, if they look a man up and down and are caught out, they just make a sarcastic remark about the man's outfit, attempting to turn it into a judgemental bitchy look instead of admitting they were mentally drooling over them. Women are far too clever for all that.

Men, on the other hand, aren't necessarily quick thinkers. They make it all too obvious what they were doing. 'No shame in their game' comes to mind. Men's eyes pop out of their head, and they become completely transfixed on their object of desire, even becoming ignorant to their wives. This is the classic tell-tale sign to any woman, and this is what gets you in trouble.

If you really cannot deny yourself the guilty pleasure of ogling at all the attractive women in the world, make sure you learn about your wife's blind spots.

Doing the 'cheeky checkout' requires a mastered skill. And I'm afraid men just don't have it.

Understanding

(That You're Wrong)

So, it's no secret that when having a lover's tiff, the man tends to back down after a while, clearly sensing his wife's irritation and seeing that there's no talking sense into her.

Women are like a dog with a bone when they feel extremely passionate about something. Men tend to give up on the argument for a quiet life, believing this will stop her shouting.

This idea is the very thing that keeps men fucking up when it comes to having a domestic. She knows you're wrong, and you know you're wrong, but to know it is not enough: she needs to hear that you're wrong. It is literally that simple to stop her shouting.

I'm sure that the majority of you reading this are baffled by how easy it is, and also shocked that you've finally found the secret you've been searching for your whole life.

Well... you're welcome.

Never tell her you've found the answer here when she becomes suspicious that you've become too marvellous at extinguishing the fire in her argument (which she will, women are suspicious creatures).

Tell her you mean it and that it's from the heart.

This will assure her that you're being genuine. You may have to undergo a few acting lessons just to perfect your performance, because in no time at all, you will be saying the now famous phrase "I was wrong, I'm sorry." Even when you know you're not wrong. It just makes life that much simpler for you, and it will satisfy her mentally.

After a while, it will become an automatic response, so be sure to listen to her words. You don't want to become ignorant now that you have the answer to your prayers. She may ask you what you want for dinner while you're watching the football. It would give the game away if your response was "I know babe, sorry, I was wrong to do that." Alarm bells would ring in her head, and you'd be under interrogation, so stay sharp and keep this book hidden under your bed.

Emotional

Women are the most emotional creatures on the planet. At least, this is what everyone assumes. The scientific truth is that men are more emotional than women. They just choose to hide it the majority of the time. Women, however, are completely clueless about this. The only rational conclusion I have come to is for you to open up to her about your feelings. Not only will this help with the amount of communication in your relationship, but she will love being able to relate to your sensitive side.

It has been proven that women find it irresistible to see a man so in touch with his emotions, and why wouldn't you open up to your wife? She should be the closest person to you. If you can't open up to her, then who can you be your true self with?

Sensitivity

We are all sensitive. It's a misconception that one gender is more sensitive than the other. Yes, that's right, perhaps we are not so different after all. And again, this is merely a case of men refusing to show their sensitivity for fear of looking unmanly, but as we previously discussed, women go crazy over a caring, sensitive man.

Never be ashamed to show your woman who you are beneath your warrior exterior. Show her the gentle giant you can be, and believe me, the response you get will be a positive one. This is beyond romance, this is beyond sex, this is raw human emotion.

Embracing all your emotions, all your feelings and all your sensitivity will only make you closer as a couple. This is the ultimate display of trust you could give her: a raw piece of your heart and letting her all the way in emotionally.

This is the greatest gift you could ever share with your partner. The weight of the world will fall off your shoulders, and she will feel closer to you, knowing how intimately she knows you inside and out. Plus, you can both better relate to one another, all the while deepening your love for each other.

Pregnancy

(Sorry pal, this is a whole other story, but I'll cover the basics!)

If you get your woman pregnant, Lord help you! If you thought a woman's emotions ran high when she's on her period, you have no idea how bad it gets when she has a bun in the oven.

Throwing up night and day, bitching about how swollen and bloated she feels. That mixed with spontaneous bursts of crying. (Good luck with that.)

But it does take two to tango, so instead of neglecting her to spend time with your friends down the pub, try staying at home and rubbing her feet.

Being randomly thoughtful goes a long way with women; they are soft, sensitive creatures that respond well to kindness.

What's typical of women is that her friends judge her. Not just by her life choices, but by the way you treat her.

The conversation goes something like this:

"God, have you seen Kelly? She's blown up like a beached whale!"

"I know. I saw her down at the supermarket doing the food shopping. ALONE."

"No! You're kidding; well, I was saying to Janet just the other day that she seems to be doing everything by herself. And where's her husband? Down the pub, getting wasted. While she's bending over the bowl vomiting all afternoon."

"How awful. I could never be with a man like that."

"She's more than likely gonna be bringing up the kid on her own."

"That's what I was gonna say. How's he gonna make a good parent when he won't look after his own wife?"

"She'll be a single parent with a wedding ring, but it won't mean a thing. Come on, we'll have to go round and help her."

That's all being said if you neglect your duties. But if you're a loving husband, here's what they'll say:

"I can't believe how much he does for her. You want to see him fetching and carrying for her like she was royalty! I'm telling you; Kelly is spoilt. She just sits there and eats, looking like the cat that got the cream. I tell you my Nile was

nothing like that. He never lifted a finger for me when I was pregnant, and he most certainly didn't take a real interest when it came to raising our daughter. He was always too busy working and drinking. I wouldn't have minded if he went out once a week or something, but it was every night. She didn't know who her bloody father was. He's still a stranger to her, even now."

"You think that's bad? My Jason didn't bother turning up when I went into labour. He stayed out playing golf with his mates. I could have killed him. Sounds like Kelly's got the perfect man."

"Tell me about it. You can tell he dotes on her. He's gonna make a great dad."

"Yeah, lucky Kelly, huh? I wish I had a man like that."

Which guy do you want to be?

Look, if you put hard work in, hard work will pay off.

If you put up with the screaming, yelling, late night crying, demanding, mood swings and the occasional blow to the head *(I kid)*, you'll be the perfect husband and father that every woman dreams about.

The better you do; the more women take it out on their husbands for not being like you. I think that's enough of a reason to be there for your wife through the tough times. Just imagine all your friends getting divorced because YOU have set the bar too high!

Sex

Sex is a crucial component in everybody's life. But the myth that men love and need sex more than women is just that: a myth.

Dare I say it, but maybe most women love it more than the majority of men? I think the reason for this is that we women have the fantastic ability to have multiple orgasms, and poor men only get to have one. And then that's it, it's all over.

Sex for him

Men experience the urge to thrust and that's about it. Men are not allowed to be selfish, because the minute he's satisfied she is still left wanting and annoyed that she hasn't had an orgasm yet *(let alone several!).*

But really think about it guys, if men could orgasm more than once in the same sex session and stay erect, wouldn't you make the most of it?

Yep, now you know how she feels.

Sex for her

Women love lots of foreplay. (P.S. great tip for men to get more involved in foreplay because you're going to satisfy her more. And you're not at risk of ejaculating all over the place and cutting the fun short.)

As well as foreplay, women love a man who can take control. Power is an aphrodisiac for women, so use that to your advantage and show her who's boss.

A catchy saying that from this moment on will always remain in your memory is:

'If your sex game is whack, she won't call you back.'

Remember that and you will go far. Practise makes perfect, and your common sense should tell you what she does and doesn't like in the bedroom, from the noises she makes. So, stay receptive. Ask questions like what her favourite position is, and don't forget to: tease, pinch, lick, suck, fuck, love, rub, hair pull, ass slap, neck bite, thrust, grab, kiss, tickle, touch, finger her, ride her, caress, and do your best.

Stick to these rules and you will have successfully satisfied your woman.

Plus, she'll brag about you to all her friends about how you are a complete sex god.

Also, when you've given your woman a good seeing to, you will see a change in the way she treats you. You may find her making you breakfast in bed, maybe a few extra kisses before work, or an erotic massage in bed. The next thing you know, she's cooking a candlelight dinner for two. You take care of her, and trust me, she'll make it up to you tenfold.

Is Bigger Better?

Yes.

If you are lacking in the genital area you can make up for it in other ways, such as foreplay and kissing.

If you're a good kisser, abuse this power because half of the work will already be done for you. She'll be wet and ready to go.

Hair pulling, neck biting, and most of all, take out the trash.

Nothing is more arousing to a woman than a man who 'helps out' round the house. Also, be a nice, sweet, and understanding man. Only men with huge genitals can be cocky (it says it all in the title).

I was also going to say men that are well endowed can act like dicks and believe they're cock of the walk (again, it is self-explanatory).

But if you are not one of the fortunate ones, then stick to what I've told you and you will be the king of your castle and be loved by your queen.

Pump, Pump, Squirt

Now I'm really gonna have to tell all men right now that this selfish act in the bedroom is inexcusable!

Remember: the woman <u>HAS TO</u> cum first.

Otherwise, she will leave you for someone who can satisfy her. So next time you need to explode, just remember the Frankie Hollywood song "Relax."

I know you think this is all very amusing, but seriously, it gets old, and you will be known as a selfish lover. There are only so many times we will accept the excuse of "I'm sorry baby, you just turn me on sooo much" or "Oh man, I couldn't help it, you're just so hot!"

Making it our fault never amuses us. And if it's the first time you have had sex together, we will get down on our knees and pray to God that it's a onetime only thing.

But if not, just know that all women talk to other women A LOT, so think twice.

Bedroom behaviour

The bedroom is known for being the place of comfort. It's also known for being the place where 'the magic happens,' as some call it. It means both for men and women, the only problem with this is knowing which time it is for the woman.

For the most part, men are perceived as sexual beasts, so if you are one of these men, let me give you some examples of when it is clearly not time to 'play' with your partner.

The Period of Her Period

This one should be self-explanatory. Bothering a woman for some hanky panky when she is feeling fat, irritable and bloated is the equivalent to prodding a lion with a sharp stick. Both will result in you losing your head.

If you do not have the kind of relationship where she openly tells you when she is experiencing the time of the month, then look out for the following signs:

> Cranky
> Snappy
> Overeating
> Rubbing her back
> Over emotional
> Barking orders
> Tossing and turning in bed all night completely unsettled

These are key signs that she's having a hell of a time with her bodily functions. Either that, or you've married a complete bitch.

After an Argument

Anything from a simple 'lover's tiff' to a full-on domestic can leave a female feeling very indifferent toward you. Just because you have both slightly calmed down, and she lets you sleep in the same bed, doesn't mean you're gonna get lucky.

You can tell from her body language when she wants nothing to do with you. She'll have her back to you, placed close to the edge of the bed to put as much distance between the two of you as possible. It is all a well thought out plan on her behalf. She wants to shut you out and let you know how cold she has become toward you.

Currently, women want nothing more than to feel love in a non-sexual way. A simple sorry and a squeeze of the shoulder should help you get back into her good books, providing what you did wasn't too terrible.

Lack of Sleep

Now, you should be able to relate to this one. This can range from your lifestyle, job, if you have children, sleeping patterns, stress - so many things can get in the way of a decent sleep, or even making sure you get enough to help you function as a regular human being. Sleep re-energises us, keeps us sane, relieves stress, and results in better mental health. Sleep is vital to us all, so if she is a mother of four, or works forty hours a week and has an incredibly stressful job, make sure you're planning to bump uglies at a decent time of the day. Pestering her just as her head finally hits the pillow won't do any favours for anyone.

Spooning

We all love to spoon. The closeness, the warmth and affection it creates brings comfort to all of us. While this is a comfy position to be in, there can be hidden meaning to it. When you are snuggling into her to steal her body heat, if she backs up into you, obviously pushing her bottom up against you, this is her not-so-subtle way of asking for some fun. So many thick-skinned men misinterpret this move and take it as her way of curling up to go to sleep, when actually this is a clear invitation to ravish her.

Disclaimer: if you do go to give her a good rodgering during spooning and she's not into it, please destroy this book, as I've clearly fucked up.

The Chase

Now we all know how complex women are. To add to man's confusion, women in the heat of an argument will say the opposite of what they mean. For extra drama, it can even transpire into a threat of them leaving and walking out on you. Here's the kicker; if she says, "Don't try to find me and never speak to me again." This is code for "you better beg and grovel at my feet to make me stay."

So many men have lost the love of their lives because they are not fluent in the language of women.

It's what's known as 'The Chase.' The chase is a common occurrence in any relationship with a woman. If you have been involved with your girlfriend/wife for quite some time now, you are already more than accustomed to her pleas for attention.

Although, there are two sides to this coin. Say you've just come back from work and found all her stuff gone. She's nowhere to be seen, and she gave you no indication that she was leaving. This means stay away. In her heart and mind, this romance has ended for her. The way to know for sure is the very fact that there were no frills, dramatics, empty threats, and no crocodile tears.

When a woman makes her oh-so-grand emotional performance of leaving you and telling you why she's going, this is her handing you an option to change her mind. Don't overlook it, don't feel defeated and believe it's hopeless trying to change her mind, because this is actually what she wants.

God, women are a puzzle! Thankfully, you have me to turn to right now, to guide you through the crazy maze of the female psyche.

But be warned, if you do not chase her and beg and plead her to stay, it just looks as though you don't care and that maybe it would be better if she did actually fuck off and never come back. At least, that's how women think. If your woman makes it out the door, in the car and off to her next destination, you're screwed! As the legendary phrase goes, 'Hell has no fury like a woman scorned.'

Given that she has left, I would say that it's game over. I dare say, at a push, if you're right behind her in the car, chasing her down the road and banging on the door, that this is at least a show of your declaration of love. But should it happen that you take to the pub to get away from all the drama, you best believe from this moment on you are officially single. No matter what your intentions are for the next day, by then it's already too late.

It's a Woman Thing

Again, another classic statement women use all the time is "I'll be five minutes." Sound familiar? That's right, whether it's said by your sister, mother, or lover each time, it means the same thing. Translated from the language of women into the language of reality; five minutes actually means anywhere between an hour to two. Men become exasperated by the time it takes for women to get ready, but surely by now you have figured out that five minutes is not an accurate amount of time for her to transform into the glam sex goddess that you know and love.

Love

Love. We love everything, we love our brother, sister, friend, song, place, thing. Anything from a favourite word to a phrase or dish, we use the word love all too frequently. Some may argue that we use this word so often that is has now lost all meaning.

Love and to be in love are two completely different things. To be in love is the highest, most intense, powerful feeling known to man. No one can obtain or control its power: you don't choose it, it chooses you.

To the true and purest form of being in love, we are powerless. We have no choice of when or where it happens, it just happens, and as we are quickly and completely consumed by love, it takes over our entire world. We, as human beings, can do nothing but sit back and enjoy the ride.

They say women fall quicker, but that men fall harder. From all the research I have uncovered, I have come to believe that this statement is true.

While the butterfly feeling in your stomach is an addictive feeling, it has to be said that relationships cannot survive on love alone.

To merely be in love with someone is not enough to guarantee you that 'happily ever after.'

To make a relationship work takes exactly that: <u>WORK!</u>

> You must work on keeping your sex life exciting.

You have to work on making quality time for each other.

You have to work on the romance.

You have to work on involving each other into each other's life.

You must work on the communication.

You have to work on your understanding of each other's dreams and aspirations.

You have to work on the trust with your partner.

But all of these apply to the pair of you.

I'm sure you're sighing with relief from this news, but it is true. This responsibility is not yours and yours alone. If you feel your woman could do with being reminded of this list, make a note of them, and give it to her. It's no good if you're making more of an effort than she is.

After all, love is a two-way street.

Marriage

The dream of the white picket fence, the kids, the dog, the perfect life is the ultimate fantasy for anyone who is in love, (sigh).

As we all know, the difference between the thrill of dating the one you love and being married to them and living with that person is vast.

We all fall victim to the fairy tale that everything will be even more amazing when we finally come to be husband and wife. The romanticised picture we have in our heads of the way things will be on our wedding day can be too tempting to resist.

Should you feel it's time to ask your love to marry you, please first consider the following before taking the plunge:

How long have you known them?

Do you know all their quirky/irritating habits?

Have you lived with this person, and if so, how long?

Do you trust this person completely?

Do you believe they love you as much as you love them?

Is it a little soon?

Think long and hard on each question. Searching for the right answers can be hard, so I'll quickly sum them up for you.

You need to have known this person for a while to know their personality, flaws, and all.

It's important to know their habits and quirky mannerisms, as the smallest thing about them can break a marriage down. You don't want to suddenly discover this person is a total freak when it's too late.

Firstly, you need - repeat NEED - to have lived with this person for at least six months to a year before even contemplating putting a ring on their finger.

Seeing each other for a few hours a day is nothing compared to constantly living in a personal space with them. The act of being perfect can be planned and put on at certain times of the day, but there will be no faking it when you both share a home. They might be ridiculously untidy/unclean or have bad mood swings or an extremely violent temper. It can be literally anything, and when you begin to live in each other's pockets, you can argue over anything. You need to see if you can even function under the same roof before declaring yourselves Mr. & Mrs.

Trust. This is a huge one. Many controlling men think that making their woman their wife will somehow tie that person to them even closer, to have more power over her and to make them feel that they own their partner. If you are riddled with doubt that your lover is being unfaithful, do NOT use marriage as a tool to monitor her every move. If you don't have trust in the relationship, it is headed for disaster. If you don't have trust, you don't have anything.

Do you know for a fact that she is as besotted with you as you are with her? If the answer is no, then don't do it. Move on and find someone who will adore you back. We all deserve the same amount of love given back to us. You should never feel less than your other half. You should never feel like she's better than you and that she's so out of your league, or you're borderline thankful that she would settle for someone like you. Feeling this way often means that you are lacking self-love and self-worth. Work on how you feel about you, become more confident and recognise your own self-worth.

To quote: 'You have to first learn to love yourself before you can expect love from another.'

Timing. Timing is key. It's fun to get caught up in a whirlwind romance, and the euphoric feeling can lead us to some hasty decisions being made all in the name of love. Don't you just hate it when someone tries to drag you back to earth when you are on cloud nine? I know I do. Many of us have experienced that friend or loved one becoming a little too vocal on our life choices, aka smoking, drinking, bad habits, and love life. We all have these people in our lives that just can't mind their own business. What we always fail to realise, though, is that they are telling us about these things for our own good. It is out of love as much as concern. So, if you hear something along the lines of "You're getting married? No way, it's too soon!" listen. Take it in. Do they have a point?

Besides, what's the rush? Clearly, if your love is true, would it really hurt to wait a year? Letting your heart rule your head is something we have all been guilty of. Whether you're using common sense or have been whisked away in a lover's dream, ultimately, the decision is yours. Either way, the outcome could still be the same; even a man with the most intelligent mind may still suffer a marriage that doesn't work out. Nothing is guaranteed in this world, but it doesn't hurt to think rationally as and when possible.

Generosity

Giving your woman trinkets and jewellery on birthdays and anniversaries is all fine and well, but shouldn't you be doing more than that? Spontaneous gestures go a long way. The occasional bunch of flowers, for absolutely no reason, is enough to keep the romance alive. As we all know, when you first start dating it is usual for the man to pay the bill at the end of dinner. However, some men are not so chivalrous. It's not at all sexy when the man is tight with his wallet strings. There has never been a faster way for a woman to harden toward you if you are the type of fuss pot that calculates what her exact half of the bill ought to be. I call these types of men 'penny pinchers,' and if you know you yourself are a penny pincher, just stay home and stay single because dating can be an expensive sport. However, there are 'penny pincher' women in this world and your frugal ways will be something of an aphrodisiac to her. She probably cooks roadkill, smells like an armpit, and reuses tampons but there is thankfully someone for everyone in this world.

Generosity should be done in moderation. There are two extremes here, either the 'penny pincher' or the 'sugar daddy;' avoid turning into either. You need to find some middle ground here. So, when does your generosity become too much?

There is a pleasure in giving, and so many rich men make the mistake of wining, dining, and bejewelling their women beyond belief. So much so, she starts to expect these lavish presents all the time. This is what is known as making her spoilt. If you've found yourself a simple country girl that was never particularly materialistic, then spoiling her is something that was done by you.

There are so many women that come pre-packaged as notorious gold diggers. There is no need to create one. There are too many of them already out there. I'm sure spending is fine if you are a billionaire and money isn't an issue for you, but for us normal nine-to-five folks, we could never provide to the level which the gold digger has become accustomed. To live beyond your means can and will eventually ruin your life. Never convince her that you have more than enough money if the opposite is true. Let her know right from the start what kind of job, money, and life you have. If that isn't good enough for her, let her walk on; you don't need a stuck-up airhead in your life. Find someone that loves you for you.

Shopping on a budget

Buying someone a gift doesn't have to be expensive. Not only are there pound shops, things on sale and great bargains out there, but never forget, a gift doesn't have to be store-bought. Some of the most romantic sentiments given have come completely free. There's a handwritten poem, picking a bunch of flowers from the garden, spending time over a hot stove to provide a thoughtfully made meal for two. You can even get creative with it, such as arts and crafts; there are many household items under your nose that could get you started off by playing together and making home-made cards or painting pictures.

They say nothing in this life is free; then how come the best feeling in life is free? Love.

Men Are No Picnic Either

By this point, you've probably left your woman and found the perfect MAN of your dreams. I'm sure you assume men are easier to deal with. Well, let me tell you, you couldn't be more wrong.

To get a better understanding of MEN, pick up my new book 'How to Keep Your MAN' out now! *Only joking.*

Men have their many hang-ups too. Everything from acting like children and being mothered by their women, to leaving every room in the house in an utter pig-sty and just assuming the house is self-cleaning. Men can be inconsiderate, lazy, and selfish. None of us are without our flaws, but when all is said and done, men and women need each other, despite all our problems. All these hang-ups can be worked on. There is no obstacle we can't overcome. If you love the person, you will make it work, no matter how difficult it is. So, before you decide to give up on women as a whole because they are too hard to live with, think about yourself for a second. Are you perfect? Are you easy to live with? Has she put up with a lot from you and loves you, regardless? Exactly. You know the answer as much as I do.

Patience, time, love, commitment, honesty and understanding make the world go round.

Congratulations! You've now completed an intense crash course on women and have no doubt learnt many valuable lessons from 'How to Keep Your Woman,' and because women are something of a puzzle, I thought it only fitting if I left you a word search of all thing's woman related. Enjoy!

Wordsearch

Can you find the following words:

*Hormones, Shoes

*Periods, Money

*Chocolate, Nails

*Cravings, Shopping

*Emotional, Hair

*Spoilt, Sex, Handbag

*Lipstick, Holidays

W	C	U	T	L	I	O	P	S	F
H	R	Z	B	P	Q	Y	K	H	T
O	A	M	O	N	E	Y	J	O	C
R	V	I	D	A	X	G	V	P	N
M	I	K	R	I	O	D	S	P	E
O	N	M	H	L	R	U	N	I	K
N	G	A	T	S	Q	W	S	N	C
E	S	X	B	J	K	Y	X	G	I
S	R	F	E	M	P	L	E	N	T
H	O	L	I	D	A	Y	S	O	S
C	H	O	C	O	L	A	T	E	P
E	M	O	T	I	O	N	A	L	I
V	G	S	Y	K	U	W	B	W	L
B	P	E	R	I	O	D	S	A	D
C	U	O	D	H	K	L	W	E	L
T	L	H	A	N	D	B	A	G	F
G	J	S	F	E	I	Y	O	J	I